PEOPLES OF THE MARITIMES

The Irish

Peter T. McGuigan

Acknowledgements

The publisher wishes to express his appreciation for the generous financial support of the **Nova Scotia Department of Tourism and Culture.**

Richard Rogers, Publisher

FOUR EAST PUBLICATIONS
P.O. Box 29
Tantallon, Nova Scotia B0J 3J0

1st edition November 1991

edited by Douglas Beall
layout and design by Paul McCormick
printed by McCurdy Printing & Typesetting Limited
cover photo courtesy of Public Archives of Nova Scotia

Canadian Cataloguing in Publication Data
McGuigan, Peter T.

    Irish

    (Peoples of the Maritimes)

    Includes bibliographical references.
    ISBN 0-0920427-32-4

1. Irish — Maritime Provinces — History.   2. Irish
Canadians — Maritime Provinces — History. *
3. Irish Canadians — Maritime Provinces —
Biography. *   4. Canada — Emigration and
immigration.   I. Title.   II. Series.

FC2050.I6M34 1991   971.5'0049162   C91-097705-4
F1035.I6M34 1991

The peoples of the Maritimes comprise in excess of seventy distinct and identifiable ethnic-cultural groups. Yet, only a few of these have their place in our history and our society well known and documented. The Peoples of the Maritimes series is an attempt to redress that imbalance by providing a well researched but readable collection of monographs for both the general and student reader.

The demographic face of Canada as a whole is changing rapidly as a result of national realities connected with the country's declining birth rate and the need for more immigrants to enhance economic growth. In this context, education and information are crucial for the promotion of harmonious social change.

The Maritimes has a rich diversity in its population, ranging all the way from the first nations and the pre-Confederation settlers to the later nation builders from all parts of the globe—more recently from Third World countries in increasing numbers. The literature on the Maritimes must keep pace with these changing times and challenges.

The Maritimes Peoples Project gratefully acknowledges the funding assistance provided for the development of this book by the Minister responsible for Multiculturalism, Government of Canada.

Bridglal Pachai, Ph.D.
General Editor

The author's thanks to:

Cyril Byrne, Saint Mary's University
Brendan O'Grady, University of Prince Edward Island
Padriag O'Siadhail, Saint Mary's University
Bridglal Pachai
Terrence Punch
Peter Toner, University of New Brunswick
Celtic Arts of Canada
Mount Allison University
National Archives of Canada
National Library of Ireland
New Brunswick Department of Tourism and Culture
Nova Scotia Department of Government Services
Provincial Archives of New Brunswick
Public Archives of Nova Scotia
Public Archives of Prince Edward Island
Saint Mary's University
Saskatchewan Archives Board
St. Francis Xavier University Archives

Peter T. McGuigan
Halifax, June 1991

TABLE OF
Contents

Chapter 1:
Whence They Came: The Homeland and the Departure
I.   The Land of Ireland 1
II.   The People of Ireland 3
III.   Religion, Population and Politics 3
IV.   Economy 4
V.   The Conquest of Ireland 5
VI.   The Penal Laws 6
VII.   A Revolutionary Time 7
VIII.   Daniel O'Connell 8
IX.   The Great Famine 9
X.   The Fenians 11
XI.   Toward the Republic 12
XII.   Northern Ireland 14

Chapter 2:
Settling In: Adjusting to the New Land
I.   The Decision to Leave 18
II.   The Voyage 20
III.   Settling In 23
IV.   Rousseau and Reality 24
V.   Religion and Irish Unity 25
VI.   The Great Famine Revisited 26
VII.   Responsible Government 27

Chapter 3:
History in the Maritimes
I.   The Orange Order 30
II.   Mid-Century 32
III.   The Exciting Sixties 33
IV.   To the Roaring Twenties 37
V.   Self-Determination 39
VI.   The Antigonish Movement 39

Chapter 4:
Contributions to the Maritimes and Canada
I.   Religion and Education 43
II.   Politics 46
III.   Business 50
IV.   Literature 50
V.   Sports 51
VI.   The Charitable Irish Societies 52

Chapter 5:
Prominent Individuals 55

Chapter 6:
Irish in the Maritimes in the 1990s 67

Bibliography 71

CHAPTER 1

Whence They Came: The Homeland and the Departure

The Irish and their descendants have played an important role in shaping life in the Maritimes. To understand the history of the Maritimes and the significance of the Irish contribution, let us begin with a look at the homeland Irish immigrants left behind.

I. The Land of Ireland

Cool, misty and green, Ireland is about 60% of the size of the three Maritime provinces. Located on the same latitudes as Labrador, but on the other side of the Atlantic Ocean, it receives the full benefit of the Gulf Stream. As a result, Ireland's climate is sufficiently mild during the winter to allow palm trees to survive in the southwest. However, its northerly location also assures that Irish summers average about 15°C, or almost 4°C cooler than in the Maritimes.

Ireland is a wet place, with an annual average of 250 or more centimetres of precipitation in the southwestern mountains and about 70 centimetres in Dublin. In contrast, the Cape Breton Highlands receive more than 160 centimetres of moisture each year, while Prince Edward Island, with 90 centimetres and considerably more summer heat than Dublin, sometimes suffers a drought. Most of the precipitation in both Ireland and the Maritimes falls as rain, but Ireland receives much less snow.

Physically, Ireland is shaped like a bowl, with a fairly low centre made up of pastures, peaty bogs and shallow lakes, all rimmed by mountains that are higher and sharper than those in the Maritime provinces. For example, Carrauntoohil in County Kerry reaches 1,014 metres above sea level, while New Brunswick's Mount Carleton is just

MAP OF
IRELAND

North
Channel

Derry
LONDONDERRY
ANTRIM

DONEGAL

Donegal
ULSTER
Belfast

TYRONE

DOWN

FERMANAGH
Armagh
ARMAGH

SLIGO
MONAGHAN

LEITRIM
CAVAN

MAYO
Westport
ROSCOMMON
LOUTH

CONNACHT
LONGFORD
MEATH

GALWAY
WESTMEATH

Athlone
Dublin
IRISH

Galway
OFFALY
KILDARE
DUBLIN

ATLANTIC
LEINSTER
SEA

OCEAN
LEIX
WICKLOW

CLARE

TIPPERARY
CARLOW

Limerick
KILKENNY
WEXFORD

LIMERICK
Cashel

Wexford

KERRY
Waterford
St. George's

MUNSTER
WATERFORD
Channel

CORK
Cork

Ireland.

Celtic Arts of Canada

820 metres. A neighbour of Great Britain, the island of Ireland is within sight of Kintyre in Scotland. And, except for Iceland, Ireland is the last major remnant of Europe to the west before Newfoundland, 3,000 stormy kilometres of ocean away.

II. The People of Ireland

The Irish are a mix of a number of groups, of which the Celts are the best known. The first inhabitants arrived from Britain about 10,000 years ago. Seven thousand years later the New Stone Age People came. They built the great passage graves such as those at Newgrange, County Meath. Later, Bronze Age Man settled, and finally about 100 B.C. the iron-using and Gaelic-speaking Celts made their appearance.

Starting with Saint Patrick in the fifth century A.D., the people of Ireland were converted from Druidism to Christianity. and for the next three or more centuries the island was a beacon of Christian civilization in Europe. Its church, the Celtic Church, was sometimes at odds with Rome but finally came into complete conformity following the Synod of Whitby held in 664.

Later, the Vikings largely destroyed the Celtic-Christian civilization, but they were in turn absorbed by the Celtic, leaving behind surnames such as Doyle and Harold and laying the foundations of towns, including Dublin and Limerick. These Scandinavians were succeeded by the Normans, those French-speaking and Scandinavian-descended Englishmen who, by using medieval technology, conquered most of the country but, like the Vikings before them, were absorbed. They provided famous Irish names such as Fitzgerald and DeCoursy. Finally came the Elizabethan English. Fired by their Protestant religion and commercial successes, they avoided absorption and so finally conquered and held the country.

Ireland was to be Britain's first and most troublesome colony. Only in 1921, after 400 years of revolution, famine and terror, did the English surrender most of the island. A free state was set up in the south, but Britain held onto part of the north, by proclaiming it the Province of Northern Ireland and there establishing a pro-British state.

III. Religion, Population and Politics

Ireland remains torn asunder with six of its thirty-two counties still in the stranger's hands. This area, Northern Ireland, is populated by a Unionist, Protestant majority that does not want to join the Republic of

Ireland. The Republic is 90% Roman Catholic, while the Province is 66% Protestant and has a much smaller population. The combined population of the two parts is about 5 million, or just slightly more than half of what it was before the Great Famine of the 1840s. In fact, Ireland is the only European country to have its population decrease by at least 50% in modern times, as a result of, as Brendan O'Grady puts it, the "twin forces of mass starvation and mass migration."

Dublin, the Republic's capital, is the largest city, with a metropolitan population of more than 800,000. Belfast, the administrative centre of Northern Ireland, is second with almost 500,000 citizens. Cork, in the Republic, is somewhat larger than Saint John and its environs.

Traditionally, Ireland has been divided into four provinces: Ulster, with six of its nine counties in Northern Ireland; Leinster, with twelve eastern counties; Connaught, made up of five western counties; and Munster, with six counties in the southeast.

The governments of the Republic and Province are parallel. Each has a Head of state—the former a president, and the latter the British monarch. In the south the government is run by a prime minister, or taoiseach, and in the north, by a provincial premier or prime minister. There are two houses of parliament in each political unit, the Republic having an elected Assembly, or Dail, and an appointed Senate, or Seanad, while Northern Ireland, with a House of Commons and Senate, also has a representative at Westminster. However, the former province has been under direct rule from London off and on since 1972, following outbreaks of violence after Catholics attempted to establish their civil rights.

IV. Economy

Many people in Ireland live in the countryside, and agriculture has employed 32% of the labourers in the Republic during recent years. The country is famous for its cattle and horses, and 90% of the agricultural land in the Republic is under hay or grass. Potatoes are still a major source of food.

In the past, Ireland was famous for the gold in County Wicklow and the copper in counties Waterford and Cork. Today, encouraged by tax concessions, prospectors have discovered deposits of lead, zinc, copper and silver. Gypsum is present in counties Cavan and Monaghan, and several types of marble are found in counties Cork, Kilkenny and Galway.

The fishing industry is underdeveloped, as it long has been—during the Great Famine, while a million or more starved, the seas were teeming with food. Today, herring, mackerel, cod, European lobster and cray-fish are taken, while the largely unpolluted rivers and lakes are fished primarily by sportsmen, yielding trout and salmon.

Some power is still supplied by traditional methods such as burning peat, but now great machines cut and stack the soggy material for drying. Some coal is mined in counties Kilkenny, Tipperary and Leitrim, but most of Ireland's energy comes from expensive imported fuels.

Manufacturing is limited. Northern Ireland has long been a manu-facturing centre, producing linen, ships (including the ill-fated *Titanic*) and, more recently, aircraft. However, these industries are being replaced by high technology, and the Republic's policy of tax conces-sions and tax-free areas (at Shannon Airport, for example) have brought their own limited rewards. Today, Ireland and Britain are closely linked economically and, unfortunately, both the Republic and Province share the economic woes of northern Britain. Therefore many people continue to leave Ireland.

V. The Conquest of Ireland

After the Norman invasion, which started in 1170 A.D., Ireland had become nominally an English colony but, slowly and inexorably, foreign control was reduced to a smaller and smaller area around Dublin. This area was called the Pale and gave rise to the expression "beyond the Pale," which came to mean "out of control" or "beyond morality."

With the Reformation, it became imperative for England to gain possession of Ireland to protect her own religious and commercial interests. England's chief rival then was Catholic Spain, and there was a danger the Spanish might invade England through the "back door" of Ireland. In 1534, Henry VIII attempted to gain control of the island by personally regranting it after his nominal governors, the House of Kildare, had rebelled. But it was his daughter, Elizabeth I, who made English control a reality. Although defeated by her armies, the Irish rose up several times. The last and most serious rebellion was that of 1595. Led by the Earl of Tyrone, Hugh O'Neill, and the Earl of Tyrconnell, Hugh O'Donnell, this final attempt to save the old Gaelic ways was lost. O'Neill beat the English at Yellow Ford in County Armagh, but he and O'Donnell and their Spanish allies were defeated at Kinsdale, County Cork, in 1601 and all hope for the old Ireland vanished.

The seed of the modern Irish problem was introduced with the British plantation of Ulster by Scottish and English Protestants, following the confiscation of O'Neill and O'Donnell's lands. The natives were displaced to inferior properties, but consequently the English and Scottish interlopers were forced to adopt a garrison mentality, ever watchful for resentful former landowners. In 1641 the reckoning came and many Protestant settlers were massacred. However, within a decade the British were back in Ireland, led by Oliver Cromwell, who had recently defeated Charles I.

Cromwell defeated the English royalists and their Irish Catholic allies by means of systematic and righteous terrorism. Drogheda's defenders and many of her citizens were put to the sword and not a priest was spared. Wexford town was attacked while trying to negotiate its own surrender, and 2,000 or more people were cut down. Cromwell then ordered all Catholic landowners to the least fertile province, Connaught. By 1714 the overwhelming Catholic majority held only 7% of the land.

Catholic hopes revived with the accession of James II to the English throne in 1685, but he was overthrown and defeated by William of Orange. James fled to Ireland and his troops besieged Londonderry (as the British called Derry town). However, English naval help arrived just as surrender was being contemplated, and the Protestants were saved. William, having become King William III, brought his troops over and defeated the royalists at the Battle of the Boyne in 1690, a victory still celebrated by the Orange Order.

VI. The Penal Laws

Protestantism had triumphed absolutely, and now it was time to force Irish Catholics into the Church of England. The tool was to be the Penal Laws, the first of which was passed five years after the British victory at the Boyne. By these laws, Catholics were not allowed to sit for parliament, join the army or even buy land. In order to break the Catholic Church, no bishops or archbishops were permitted, so that the priesthood might die out through a dearth of ordinations. As well, any son who turned Anglican could inherit all of his family's estate. Ultimately, however, these regulations failed through a mixture of irregular enforcement by government and a bending of the rules by sympathetic or corrupt officials.

Another aspect of the Penal Laws was the infamous Anglican Tithe, by which even those who did not adhere to the Church of England were forced to pay for its support. The Tithe also irritated the Presbyterian settlers of Ulster and many of them fled during the eighteenth century to America and became staunch anti-British rebels during the American Revolution.

VII. A Revolutionary Time

The late eighteenth century was a revolutionary time, and Ireland played her role in the action. The first modern Irish nationalists were those of the Protestant Ascendency, noted more for their Georgian mansions and great estates than for making trouble. However, feeling imposed upon by London, they wanted an independent parliament. Thus, during the American Revolution, they organized a militia to guard Ireland while the redcoats were busy in America, and they then demanded, in return, a local parliament. Britain gave in out of a mixture of fear and appreciation, and an Irish assembly was authorized in 1782. However, England kept the real power to herself through her control of patronage and the buying of seats, and the Ascendency was left holding an empty bag.

The American Revolution was a serious blow to the British Empire, but the French Revolution of 1789 shook the very foundations of Western civilization. Seeing the Catholic Church as an ally against French excesses, Britain finally granted concessions in Ireland. Catholics were allowed to buy some land, join most ranks in the military and in 1795 even obtained help to found Maynooth Seminary, a priest's training school. However, Catholics were still not allowed to sit in parliament or to avoid the Tithe.

Despite these changes, revolutionary ideas spread to Ireland. Wolfe Tone, a Dublin Protestant, became the best known of the so-called United Irishmen. This organization tried to join Catholics and Protestants to establish an Irish republic. Receiving help from revolutionary France, in 1798 the United Irishmen attempted to land forces at Bantry Bay, County Cork, but failed because of contrary winds, and this rebellion was nipped in the bud. A number of Ulster Presbyterians had risen in support of Tone but were defeated and massacred by Irish Catholic soldiers of the Royal Army, while the rising in Wexford disintegrated into a peasant's revolt accompanied by revenge slayings of Protestant bigots and Irish Catholic soldiers who protected them. (The soldiers pleaded for their lives in Irish, a language the Wexford people no longer understood.)

This was also the time of the formation of the Orange Order. This Ulster-based, anti-Catholic organization was largely supported by peasants and small merchants and was of Low-Church Anglican persuasion. It opposed the United Irishmen and set out to drive the Catholics from County Amagh. The Order has been the backbone of Unionist resistance in the north ever since.

The United Irishmen's ship had foundered on the rocks of sectarianism, and the Irish parliament voted itself out of existence after accepting hefty bribes, so the political situation returned to "square one." The modern Irish pattern had begun to emerge—concessions to Catholics would draw increased resistance from most of the pro-British minority and especially from the Unionist majority in Ulster.

VIII. Daniel O'Connell

The rise of Daniel O'Connell changed the ideal of Irish nationalism from an ecumenical vision to a Roman Catholic one. This County Kerry lawyer was dedicated to the emancipation of his people and to the repeal of parliamentary union with England. Elected from County Clare in 1828, as a Roman Catholic he could not sit. However, his use of the Catholic Association's disciplined and sober masses forced England in 1830 to concede through fear what it would not through justice—what became known as the Catholic Emancipation. As a result, Catholics throughout the Empire were allowed to take their seats in their respective legislatures.

Irish emancipation had been accomplished rather quickly, but O'Connell's goal to revive an Irish parliament was not to be. Westminster simply had no intention of granting real independence to Dublin, as she had already demonstrated with her sham concessions to the Ascendency in 1782. However, O'Connell, unseeing, organized a series of "Monster Meetings" following his failure to gain sufficient reforms through alliance with English political parties. A series of repeal of the union petitions was organized around the world, including in the Maritimes. However, when the British government outlawed a great repeal gathering at Clontarf, County Dublin, in October 1843, O'Connell cancelled the assembly and his movement collapsed. In any case, it was too late. O'Connell, later released from jail, was a dying man and Ireland herself was about to become deathly ill, for the Great Famine was at hand.

IX. The Great Famine

For decades the population of Ireland had been growing out of control, especially among those least able to support themselves, the landless peasants. These people had been able to feed their families on tiny rented potato plots, at least in the good years. However, even in these "good" years, more than one-quarter of the Irish were malnourished. Famines had occurred before. For example, in 1817 many had died, but the illiterate peasants continually hoped for just one more good crop of potatoes which, when in the pot, "smiled back at ye."

By 1841, at least 8 million people were reported to live in Ireland, and because of under-reporting, the actual total may have been closer to 11 million. In the autumn of 1845 an unknown disease suddenly struck. Tubers that were good one week became a rotten and stinking waste the next. Various "cures" were attempted and the infection was blamed on everything from lightning to easterly winds. The cause was actually a fungus, *Phytophthora infestans*, whose wind-borne spores spread throughout the island.

What was the British government to do? Theoretically, Ireland was part of the United Kingdom of Britain and Ireland. Irishmen sat in the House of Commons and even in the House of Lords, and they paid the hated Tithe, although with great reluctance. However, the Irish were generally regarded by the English as inferior, superstitious, dirty and ignorant. This attitude, and the government's absolute faith in the free market system, meant that its response was to be much less than what union should have meant, and amounted to a series of knee-jerk reactions rather than a consistent policy.

In late 1845 the prime minister, Sir Robert Peel, imported large amounts of maize (Indian corn) and eventually planned to sell it from depots at low cost to the Irish. By the next spring, Peel had helped to set up a series of public works to provide the peasants with enough money to buy the food. He had also revoked the corn laws (which had inhibited the importation of grains) in order to lower the price of bread. This was a good start, given the attitudes of capitalists who felt that the market would be undermined by the distribution of free food and that shortages and unnecessary suffering would result.

However, the application of these laws became the immediate problem. The Indian corn depots were closed far too quickly in the false hope of a good 1846 harvest. And, through bureaucratic inefficiency, payment for public employment was so delayed in some cases that

Irish emigrants arrive at Cork: a scene on the quay.

workers starved to death. About 140,000 people were employed in public works that wound up on August 1846. However, with the dismal harvest that followed, the public works were restarted that autumn and by Christmas supported 400,000 men, who each represented on average four other people. As a result, 2 million lives were being saved, at least for the time being. But how many were not?

By March 1847 almost 750,000 people were employed in public works. The British government finally gave in to the enormous pressure from the starving unemployed and started to distribute free rations from soup kitchens. By late summer 1847 more than 3 million people were begging for food and the British government, terrified by the apparent threat to the free market, closed the soup kitchens, leaving tens of thousands to die. The government's excuse had been the appearance of a small but good potato harvest in the autumn of 1847. The British declared the problem solved, even though infections had been spreading for more than a year. Parliament had amended the Poor House Act to allow non-residents to work within their confines, but the tax rates to support them were so high that even prosperous Irish landlords were faced, in some cases, with ruin. The burden had been shifted from the English government to the Irish people.

The leaving now began in desperation. In May 1847, 100,000 Irish were wandering the streets of Liverpool, England, waiting for a chance to sail to "Amerikay." Some would reach the Maritimes that summer and autumn, especially Saint John.

The winter of 1847-48 was, to make things worse, one of most bitter on record. The years 1848 and 1849 were the worst years of the famine. Without sufficient help the Irish had no choice but to flee in greater and greater numbers. At least 1.5 million (and possibly as many as 2 million) had left Ireland by 1851, and at least one million or possibly twice that number died of starvation and disease. It is no wonder that Ireland's officially expected population of more than 9 million fell almost 2.5 million short in the 1851 census.

X. The Fenians

One expression of accumulated Irish bitterness toward Britain was the Fenians. Organized by James Stephens, a Protestant radical, this organization was named the Irish Republican Brotherhood in Ireland, but its American branch was called the Fenian Brotherhood, and this is the name by which it became known. The American Civil War gave the Fenians their baptism of fire and by 1865 they were ready to strike at Britain in Ireland. However, their plot was discovered and Stephens was jailed. He soon escaped and began to organize another rebellion the next year, but he eventually called off the action and was deposed by an American Civil War veteran, Colonel T.J. Kelly. A small number of Americans then sailed with Kelly to Dublin from New York City, but their March 1867 revolt was discovered and Kelly was captured. He too escaped, but a British policeman was killed in the process. Three Irishmen, none of whom had fired the shot, were hung, thus becoming the "Manchester Martyrs."

XI. Toward the Republic

For a decade after the Fenian defeat, Ireland was quiet. However, in the late 1870s agrarian unrest again appeared. The opening of the American West had cut the market for wheat and this combined with a failure in the potato crop, lead to fears of a return of famine. In 1879, the Land League was formed to stop landlords' evictions. Certain members of the league began to assassinate proprietors and to organize boycotts. The British prime minister, William Ewart Gladstone, responded using a carrot and stick approach. A land act that set up rent tribunals and legalized the "Ulster custom" of selling the lease to the highest bidder was enacted in 1881. As well, a Coercion Bill that inflicted severe penalties on resistors and suspended some civil liberties was passed. These two acts took the wind from the sails of the Land League and their ship was becalmed.

Land reform continued into the early twentieth century with two more acts. In 1903 and 1909, legislation was approved that forced proprietors to sell to their tenants. This legislation, combined with Gladstone's disestablishment of the Anglican Church in 1869, left one major remaining problem—the political relationship of Britain and Ireland.

In 1886 Gladstone proposed his first Home Rule bill, which would have given Ireland a status similar to Canada's at the time. However, this bill was defeated when his Liberal party split over the issue. Gladstone's second attempt to introduce a similar measure was vetoed by the House of Lords after threats of armed resistance in Ulster.

Almost a generation later, in 1911, the Liberals had returned to power but needed the support of the Irish Nationalists, and so stripped the Lords of their veto. The following year the Liberals introduced a third Home Rule bill. This bill seemed certain to pass, but a resulting civil war in Britain was feared. The Unionists of Ulster, overwhelmingly Protestant, were arming with the help of the English Conservative party and elements of the Royal Army to resist the will of the freely elected British parliament. However, the outbreak of the First World War in August 1914 delayed the confrontation, and the Home Rule bill passed quietly into law the next month. Irishmen, both Catholic and Protestant, marched off to the slaughter, believing on the one side that the legislation would be implemented as passed and on the other side that Ulster would be excluded from Home Rule,

The Easter 1916 uprising in Dublin was totally unexpected by both the British and the Irish. A group of extremists, some obsessed with the need for a blood sacrifice paralleling that of Christ, decided to establish a republic through force. However, after a week of fighting they were defeated. Following an excessive number of executions, the Irish public's indifference toward the rebels turned into sympathy and the killings were stopped. With the release of the two most dynamic survivors, Eamon de Valera and Michael Collins, that feeling was channeled into political victory for Irish nationalists. In the December 1918 British elections, De Valera and Collins' party, Sinn Fein, won handily and almost immediately declared a republic. Britain simply ignored them, but Collins was not to be denied and ordered the military wing of Sinn Fein, the Irish Republican Army (IRA) to assassinate British police. Soon after, Britain lost control and released the "Black and Tans," tough veterans of the First World War, who burned the centre of Cork city, shot its pro-republican mayor and then opened fire on a crowd watching an Irish football game in Dublin, killing thirteen. The IRA responded, but by December 1921 a stalemate in terror had occurred and Britain and Ireland signed a peace treaty that set up the Irish Free State. This treaty was theoretically supposed to apply to the entire island, but in fact a separate parliament had been set up in Belfast five months earlier. Furthermore, the Free State was not as free as the Dominion of Canada, and Irishmen still had to swear allegiance to the British monarch, George V. The Home Rule treaty had been interpreted to exclude Ulster.

Furthermore, Collins had signed the treaty without final consultation with De Valera, and as a result the republicans split and De Valera led the IRA against his former comrades, now the Irish government. Collins was assassinated in August 1922, but the next year, lacking sufficient support from the war-weary Irish public and facing draconian legal measures, De Valera told his men to abandon their arms. The Irish Civil War thus ended with Northern Ireland intact as a British province and the Free State still owing fidelity to George V. Nothing had been gained by all the bloodshed.

After a short term in jail, De Valera was elected to the Dail and in 1932 led his party to victory, determined to create a republic as soon as politically expedient. He refused to pay the land annuities owed to Britain from the forced sale of landlords' Irish estates early in the century, and this led to an economic war. However, in 1938, Britain and Ireland signed a treaty that gave the latter possession of the remaining English military bases on the island. (This concession later restricted Britain's action against Nazi U-boats.) De Valera also stripped the governor general of all his powers, and so Ireland became a republic in all but name.

De Valera kept the Free State out of the Second World War, but hundreds of thousands of its citizens, along with Unionists from Northern Ireland, fought against the Nazis. De Valera was finally defeated in 1948 and the new prime minister, John Costello, after being insulted in Ottawa by Ulster-born Canadian Governor General Viscount Alexander of Tunis, finally declared southern Ireland a republic.

XII. Northern Ireland

The 1921 act that had set up the Northern Ireland enclave was supposed to promote proportional representation of Protestants and Catholics, but this balance was abolished as early as 1922. Britain had done nothing to enforce the legislation. Sectarian riots followed in the 1920s and 1930s and systematic discrimination continued against a largely pro-Republican Catholic minority for decades thereafter. Not until the 1960s did members of this minority, inspired by Martin Luther King's civil rights marches in the southern United States, try to regain full status as British citizens in Northern Ireland.

The Orange response was unfortunately predictable. The marchers were attacked by both civilians and police, and the Irish Catholic enclave of the Bogside in Londonderry was savaged. British troops were brought in to stop the bloodshed and maintain English rule. This intervention gave the IRA a chance to come out of the shadows after almost half a century of irrelevancy. Assassinations of British soldiers resumed, this time in Belfast rather than in Dublin or Cork. Internment of suspects followed and, in January 1972, British troops opened fire on civil rights marchers in Londonderry, killing thirteen. These events were followed by the 1974 Ulster Protestant workers' strike that destroyed the power-sharing agreement made the previous year between the Republic and Britain. A situation reminiscent of the seventeenth century had arisen and continues.

Ireland has absorbed the Vikings, taken in the Normans and largely got rid of the English, but how will Northern Ireland become part of the Irish nation as long as the past cannot be forgotten?

CHAPTER 2
Settling In: Adjusting to the New Land

In 1759 the Maritimes were rapidly reverting to wilderness. The Acadian Expulsion, which had started in 1755, had left the Annapolis Valley, the Truro area, the New Brunswick-Nova Scotia border country and the Hillsborough River area of Prince Edward Island virtually deserted. The great fortress at Louisbourg had just fallen for the second and last time and was being demolished, its 4,000 former inhabitants scattered into exile.

Only Halifax, with less that 2,000 people, and Lunenburg were left as significant centres of European settlement. As the major Britsh outpost in the Maritimes, Halifax had a social structure similar to the military and governmental towns in Ireland, and a tiny and part-Irish Protestant ruling class lorded over a much larger group of riff-raff that included a slowly and irregularly growing Irish Catholic population. This illiterate mass was to have a profound effect not only on the town but on the future of Canada.

The Seven Years' War ended in 1763 with the French ceding Cape Breton, Prince Edward Island and New Brunswick to Britain. This entire area was to be part of Nova Scotia until 1769, when Prince Edward Island broke away, followed fifteen years later by New Brunswick and Cape Breton. However, finding independence difficult, Cape Breton rejoined Nova Scotia in 1820.

The very first Irish in the Maritimes had come during the 1600s and scattered over Acadia and nearby Newfoundland. After 1713, when Louisbourg was constructed, a significant number of Hiberians settled there. An Irish priest, Timothy Lynch, was a missionary at the fort during the 1740s, and in the next decade a number of Catholics from the

Irish emigrants leaving home: the priest's blessing.

Nova Scotia mainland and Newfoundland sought refuge there from discrimination. Newfoundlanders also sailed to the fortress to have their children baptized or their marriange regularized. But only after the collapse of the French empire in North America did the real story of permanent Irish settlement in the Maritimes begin.

I. The Decision to Leave

Irish grievances boiled down to their reduction to strangers in the own land, a feeling that was shared to some extent by Protestants who had been planted in Ulster several generations before. Power was in the hands of the British parliament in London and, as previously mentioned, the attempt by the Protestant Ascendancy to establish an Irish parliament in Dublin had come to naught. The Penal Laws had come close to breaking the Catholic Church, and trade restrictions, as well as the failure of Ireland to industrialize, left the inhabitants as hewers of wood and drawers of water. Finally, uncontrolled population growth and irregular but recurrent crop failures drove many to leave before it was too late.

Where could the Irish go? Their choices were largely restricted to two: the overcrowded but industrializing cities of Britain or the daunting

Emigrants leaving home in the west of Ireland.

wilderness of North America. At one time or another Britain held the entire American coast from just north of Florida to as far as Newfoundland and, with the Native population being decimated by disease and pushed back by European conquest, space was becoming available.

How far the Irish sailed depended on several factors, money being the major one. Many were too poor to go beyond the Maritimes, at least initially. Eventually, about half of the Irish arrivals would leave for "the land of the free and the home of the brave." Sometimes they arrived because of other factors. Sometimes shipowners would make false statements about the length of the passage, enabling them to extract the last of the immigrants' savings by charging exhorbitant prices for food toward the end of the voyage. At other times immigrants were simply misled, like those who thought they were sailing to Charleston, South Carolina, but ended up in Charlottetown, Prince Edward Island, instead.

Sometimes Irish emigrants were attracted by farmland. Such was the case of the settlers brought from Ireland and New England during the 1760s by Alexander McNutt. These were Ulster Scots who took over the Acadian farms in the Truro area, and those in the Tantramar marshes on the New Brunswick-Nova Scotia border. The Ulster Catholics, or Monaghan Settlers, who went to Prince Edward Island in the 1830s and 1840s were encouraged by priests in Ireland and on Prince Edward Island. Partially as a result, Prince Edward Island, which was to have no Catholics, ended up with almost half of its settlers being adherents of Rome.

In Cape Breton those who came because of the discovery of a large hill of very good coal at Sydney Harbour helped form the "Irish Grant" between Low Point and Glace Bay. Others came for less positive reasons. Mogue Doyle, a veteran of the 1798 rebellion in Ireland, fled to Cape Breton after escaping from prison dressed in his wife's clothing. Initially he stayed with his uncle, Lawrence Kavanaugh, in Arichat. Then when sufficient time had passed he returned to County Wexford, cleared his name and finally sailed back to Cape Breton. Several of his descendents became clergy, including one who became an archbishop of Milwaukee, Wisconsin.

During the 1820s others from the south of Ireland were attracted to the relatively prosperous cities of Saint John and Halifax. In Halifax, for example, where the waterfront was being reconstructed, the Shubenacadie Canal was being built and a quarter-century-long renovation of the Citadel was beginning, the unlettered immigrant could find work.

Finally, the opening of the forest industry in the Miramichi to help the British replace the lumber lost as a result of Napoleon's blockade of the Baltic led many Irish Catholics to settle, where they gained a reputation for pugnacity and maintained the Irish language for many years. Thousands of Miramichi Irish later emigrated to the United States and to Ontario, following the lumbering trade, when the protective tariffs that had led to the New Brunswick lumber boom were withdrawn.

II. The Voyage

The leaving of Ireland, painful as it was, was tempered by the hope of a secure future, but only after a trial of weeks and weeks in a rolling ship. The trip itself could range from a boring passage with a peaceful outcome to a peaceful passage with a tragic outcome, as shown by the following accounts.

To escape his creditors in Ireland, Father William Phalen sailed to Halifax in the spring of 1786. He left London on March 13th and entered into a low-key adventure. During this time the priest wrote to his bishop, justifying his sudden and unauthorized departure, and told of his

On board an immigrant ship.

voyage. Phalen paid eight guineas, something over £8, for a relatively comfortable steerage berth on the *Mary*, commanded by John Wright. Despite his lowly circumstances, he was invited to the captain's table at least once. There he sized up the commander as a vain but intelligent man and used the blarney to keep relations running smoothly.

The food varied considerably depending upon the price of the accommodation. The cabin class had delicacies such as tongue and fowl, butter, cheese, tea, coffee and chocolate. And there was wine and porter to wash it down. Phalen's class made do with beef, potatoes, dumplings and beer. But when fresh meat ran out, they ate (on a three-day cycle) watered mess beef and potatoes, followed by watered mess beef and dumplings and then by watered mess pork with peas, soup and potatoes. They had to supply their own sugar and porter, and some were well supplied with the latter.

Phalen's passage took a tedious nine weeks and two days and he complained, apparently without justice, that other ships had left London one or two weeks later and arrived in Halifax seven to fourteen days earlier than he had. Delaying his own passage, however, was a storm that drove the *Mary* two knots east despite all sails being furled. Temperatures also varied remarkably. Until April 26th it was cold. Then east of Newfoundland, with southerly winds, the temperature suddenly became pleasant. However, on May 3rd, they sailed into northwesterly winds and the air became cold and foggy. Nine days later, as they neared Sable Island, five "hallobits" (halibuts) were caught which, with cod obtained the next day, made up at least in part for the pig, geese and fowl that had washed overboard when the *Mary* shipped heavy seas. Ten leagues off Halifax, Phalen counted forty American fishing boats. When he finally arrived in port on May 17th, he was greeted by a number of trustees of St. Peter's Roman Catholic Church who had been checking every ship in anticipation of the arrival of a priest, and so ended his boring but peaceful voyage.

The famine voyages during "Black '47" were not boring but tragic. British landlords saw a chance to "shovel out" their paupers and dump the burden on the poor and underdeveloped colonies, and Saint John received more than its share during the summer of 1847. On May 31st, Sir Robert Gore-Booth's ship *Aeolus* arrived in the New Brunswick port from County Sligo with 500 of his most indigent tenants. He had kindly given them a one-way passage from their ancestral land. When they reached Saint John, there was no sickness, but soon infection appeared. Two weeks later, Michael Driscoll, captain of the *Aeolus*, wrote a fawning letter to Gore-Booth talking of the latter's kindness in sending the tenants away from starvation. He also told of the good treatment they had received upon arrival in Saint John, of all the girls being sent to respectable homes, of the plentiful employment and of the *Aeolus* being superior to Her Majesty's transports in accommodation.

In contrast to this missive was a letter from another shipper's agent, John Robertson. He had heard that Gore-Booth was preparing to dump another load of paupers via the *Yeoman* and protested, telling of how the Irish had had to underbid others to get any work at all and then, as they became dissatisfied with their low wages, made trouble. This letter was of no use, for the next month the *Yeoman* sailed into Saint John with another load of starving Irishmen.

On November 1st, the last day the quarantine station was open the returned *Aeolus* appeared on the horizon. Chartered this time by Lord Palmerston, it carried 428 more County Sligo destitutes, many of whom would never see Christmas. Included were feeble men and aged widows. The officials were oputraged, but attempts to pay the indigents' way back to Ireland were not accepted. Thus the city was left with hundreds of more welfare cases by a man who later was to become the prime minister of Britain and Ireland.

III. Settling In

Father Phalen's letter also provides a view of Halifax in 1786. This major British American settlement, then in its fourth decade, had 6,000 inhabitants. The harbour was described as safe and spacious and less prone to fog than the immediate offshore. Two formidable batteries stood at its entrance, and across the water in Dartmouth a great number of houses were being constructed for the Quaker whalers who had fled Nantucket Island, Massachusetts, because of the trade war between the newly freed United States and Britain.

The settlement ran from the harbour's edge, up rising ground to the Citadel and was described as smaller than Kilkenny but larger than Carlow. Its houses were small, wooden and painted white. For miles around the forests had been burned to protect the settlement against Indians. Phalen also stated that, despite the poor and rocky soil, a fine crop of wheat and potatoes grew that could be harvested before those in his cool and misty former homeland.

Halifax had been the only British dockyard in the Americas not taken during the American War of Independence, but now with peace there was little trade or money in this military port. Most imports came from England for which Halifax traded fish, lumber, furs, beef, and potatoes. However, there was a glut of fish, especially cod, lobster and herring, and West Indian produce was available at reasonable cost even though the trade war with the United States had made other prices too dear.

The small Irish Catholic group in Halifax had joined with the even smaller Irish Protestant population to form the Charitable Irish Society. This group was designed to dispense aid to the needy and to provide its members with entertainment in a quiet town. The Catholics had just finished their first church, St. Peter's. Phalen thought the chapel was rather large for the congregation and that the arrangement of pews and galleries made it look like a Protestant house of worship. He also did not like the Acadian chants and was curious about the excessive length of the mass. The pastor, Father James Jones, explained that the mass was being lengthened to attain some equality with the services of other denominations.

IV. Rousseau and Reality

Loneliness was the lot of pioneers, whether rual or coastal, and their work was backbreaking. However, the romantics of Rousseau's era saw the pioneer as a natural man; a noble savage. Such a dreamer was Lord Edward Fitzgerald, who in 1798 would be shot as an Irish rebel while resisting arrest. Ten years earlier he had travelled through southern New Brunswick and described to his mother the Irish he found there. Fitzgerald stated that they had come without a shilling and were now worth £1,000 to £3,000. Even better, he said, there were no gentlemen, but only an industrious class that had by its labout attained the perfection of man. Passing a cabin on a hot forenoon, he was so moved by the thought that one family had settled 20 miles upstream that he thought he might never return home. Unfortunately, for his life, he did.

In contrast to this romantic view was that of Father François Lejamtel of Arichat. Lejamtel had led his people from St. Pierre and Miquelon to Cape Breton to avoid the excesses of the French Revolution. His new parish, mostly Acadian with a significant number of Irishmen, consisted mainly of fishermen and poor farmers. In a letter written in 1807 to his superior in Quebec City, he discussed the abuse of alcohol. It tended to flow like water, he wrote, and even children had access to it. The results were the infamous Saturday night frolics, festivities marked by intoxication, fighting and undue familiarity between the sexes. The priest received little satisfaction from his efforts to reform the parishioners, and not until the 1830s, when Father Theobald Mathew's temperance crusade swept Ireland with 2 million registrants, was much progress made in fighting this tendency among the Irish on either side of the Atlantic.

V. Religion and Irish Unity

Religion was often a divisive factor both within and between denominations. In Saint John, the Ulster Scots were not satisfied with the liberality of St. Andrew's Presbyterian Church and in 1842 when a ministerial vacancy occurred they tried to install their own man. Led by William Parks, they contacted the moderator of the Presbyterian Church in Ireland, but the Scots countered with the opinion of St. Andrew's founder that no members of the synod of Ulster could lead the congregation even though the churches in Scotland and Ireland were in communion. As a result, many of the Irish left and founded the St. John's Presbyterian Church in the same city.

The Catholics had come close to splitting over a different issue forty years earlier in Halifax. The dispute had been trusteeism, or who controlled the parish, the founders or the priest. In 1781 a number of the newly elected, middle-class parishioners petitioned George III for relief from two of the provisions of the 1759 anti-papist legislation passed by the Nova Scotia Assembly. These laws had placed restrictions on the practice of the Catholic faith and on the ownership of land by its members. Within two years the British ruler approved the revocation of the statutes.

The same group then built the first Catholic church in Halifax and in 1785, acting on their own initiative, brought Father James Jones from Ireland as pastor. Having accomplished all this, they then felt they could tell the priest how to run the church, creating a situation that led to years of bitter relations. For example, the trustees criticized Jones for leasing part of his underutilized presbytery, threatened to sue him for supposedly misusing part of the missionary fund and even interfered in strictly ecclesiastical affairs when they disinterred a suicide who had repented on his deathbed. The priest's second successor, Irish-born Edmund Burke, finally brought the trustees under control. However, it was not until 1842 that these self-righteous men gave up their lease on the church property.

VI. The Great Famine Revisited

Generally Irish immigrants had been welcome, especially if they were young, healthy and had sufficient money. However, most of those who fled during the Great Famine had not even one of those attributes, so not only were they not welcome, but if possible they were sent back to Ireland.

The famine affected the Maritimes in two significant ways. Hordes of destitute and diseased people swamped Saint John and other places and the potato rot affected Prince Edward Island and, especially, Cape Breton. During "Black '47" only one famine ship appeared off Prince Edward Island, the *Lady Constable* from Liverpool, England, with 25 dead out of 440. Things were worse in the Miramichi region of New Brunswick where the *Looshtauk* from Dublin came in with 175 dead and 96 dying, before sailing on to Gros Isle, Quebec, where the ship dropped more dead and dying.

However, Saint John took the brunt. This port of 30,000 people was left with almost 15,000 strangers, many of whom were old, sick or crippled. The quarantine station on Partridge Island saw its first coffin ship on May 5, 1847, when the *Midas* from Galway left 10 dead out of 163. Eleven days later, the *Aldebaran* of Sligo, which had already lost 36, unloaded 382 living, of whom 80 would soon pass away. On May 22nd the *Pallas* from Cork brought 204 living and one dead; soon, however, 27 more, including the captain, would die.

So it went all summer. In May and on June 4th, 893 arrived. July brought 4,058, but then the flood began to ease off. August had 3,509, September 1,380 and October 1,052.

Partridge Island's 24 acres were the first and last North American home to many of these immigrants. Temporary sheds were built, but they were unheated, without floors and overcrowded. The situation became so bad that tents made of ship's sails had to be pressed into service, and conditions were ripe for infection. Typhus and relapsing fever spread and the effect was magnified by a lack of physicians who dared to step on the island. The one well became polluted, and the only spring dried up in summer. The healthy were forbidden to leave the place for fear of spreading the diseases, and so tended to come down with them. It is no wonder that one of the immigrants from the norotious *Aeolus* said that it was almost as bad as Ireland.

The fungus *Phytophthora infestans* that had devastated Ireland's crops also affected the Maritimes during the 1840s. As early as 1843 the infection attacked Cape Breton's potato crop, and it continued on parts of the island for the rest of the decade. As a result, in 1846 the Nova Scotia government reluctantly doled out £3,667 for the colony. Despite the unenthusiastic allotments, the death toll mounted and Cape Breton became known as "The Ireland of Nova Scotia." More would have perished but for the actions of merchants such as Dublin-born Peter Smyth. he had come to Cape Breton in 1832 and eventually had become a successful businessman in the Port Hood area. During the famine he gave food on credit, no matter how remote the possibility of repayment. As a result, in 1847 he was elected as the member of the colonial legislature for Inverness County.

With substitute crops and drier weather, the agricultural problems eventually disappeared on Cape Breton, but the island's population did not recover until the twentieth century.

VII. Responsible Government

Representative government, the form of administration by which geographically defined groups of people have a spokesman in an assembly, became the law in Nova Scotia in 1758. However, the franchise was narrow and excluded the poor, Blacks, women and Catholics. However, by the 1840s, with the adoption of a wider franchise, which now included many Catholics freed by the 1830 Emancipation Act, the call came for "responsible government," a form of administration where the executive, or cabinet, would be dependent on the support of elected members. This system was already in place in Britain and the colonists saw no reason why they should not follow suit.

The fight was led by the Liberal party of Nova Scotia. However, great tension developed within the party during the struggle, as one movement, Repeal (of the union of Britain and Ireland), tended to split the organization and the other, Responsible Government, tended to unite it. Most apparent was the conflict between the two most prominent leaders—the famous reformer Joseph Howe and the self-assured Irish repealer Lawrence O'Connor Doyle. O'Connor Doyle had helped to form the Loyal Repeal Association in 1847, and it had spread rapidly, reaching Saint John, Sydney and Prince Edward Island that year. On P.E.I. it was also seen as part of the struggle against the landlords, and so it attracted many non-Irish.

Howe was a staunch imperialist despite his liberal leanings. Like many Protestants, he felt the words *loyal* and *repeal* were contradictory, and he was also personally opposed to O'Connor Doyle. He was even prepared to delay the implementation of responsible government and had advised Catholics to vote against Doyle. They had ignored him, and both men had been elected as Liberals in 1843. However, two seats short of a majority, the party had to settle for the Opposition.

Four years later, with the next election, growing sectarianism became a bigger threat to the Liberals. the Tory *Times* wrote darkly of a threat to Protestant Nova Scotia from the rising Catholic tide, especially in view of the 1,200 famine victims who had arrived in Halifax that summer. However, despite this sentiment, the Liberals swept to victory with the help of the Irish in Halifax who again elected both O'Connor Doyle and Howe. The first responsible government in the overseas British Empire was formed in Nova Scotia on February 2, 1848.

So ends the story of the Maritime Irish up to the middle of the nineteenth century. Almost all of those who would come to the Maritimes had now arrived. Even in New Brunswick the majority had come before the famine. The attempt to repeal the union of Britain and Ireland had almost irrevocably split the Irish into Orange and Green, both here and back in Ireland. And so it would remain for the next century, until sectarianism was replaced by secularism, and religion faded as an important day to day force.

CHAPTER 3
History in the Maritimes

The Irish who settled in the Maritimes during the second quarter of the nineteenth century varied in their religions, geographical origins, settlement patterns and proportions within local Maritime populations.

Religiously, the Prince Edward Island Irish were the most homogeneous, being overwhelmingly Roman Catholic. Those in New Brunswick had almost equal numbers of Protestants and Catholics, while Nova Scotia's Irish were closer to Prince Edward Island's religious proportions.

Nova Scotia's Irish were the most uniform in geographical origins, having come mostly from within 90 kilometres of the Irish port of Waterford and the western part of Munster. However, many also had come from the hinterland of the port of Londonderry. Prince Edward Island and New Brunswick's Irish were more mixed in their origins. Like Nova Scotia, P.E.I. had a base of southeastern and southern Irish, but also a thick layer of County Monaghan settlers who had largely come through the port of Belfast. The New Brunswick Irish came from the hinterlands of three ports—Belfast, Londonderry and Cork—a fact that hints at their religious preferences.

New Brunswick had four major concentrations of Irish settlement: Saint John, the Saint John River Valley, Charlotte County and the Miramichi Valley. In Prince Edward Island, the Irish were located in farming communities, especially in the Queens County/Prince County border area and in Charlottetown. Nova Scotia's Irish dwelled mostly near Truro, in Halifax, in Guysborough County, in the "Irish Grant" in Cape Breton and in the Margaree Valley.

Although Nova Scotia was only 15% Irish, almost 20% of Sydney's population and 25% of Halifax's people claimed such origins. On Prince Edward Island one-quarter of the settlers were from the Emerald Isle, but more than 40% of Charlottetown's people were. In New Brunswick, where one out of three were Irish, the proportion rose at its high point to four out of ten in the Miramichi and to six out of ten in Saint John.

I. The Orange Order

The Orange Order has been called, among other things, the greatest organization formed by the Irish. Established in the mid-1790s in County Armagh, the organization protected the superior Protestant position in the border country, where Catholics nearly equaled non-Catholics in number.

Attractive to Low-Church Anglicans, the members of the Orange Order practiced sobriety and welfare and sought to convert Catholics, who they felt were misled by "dark clerical forces." The royal family was honoured and the great Protestant victory at the Battle of the Boyne was celebrated each July 12th. The Orange organization tended to be egalitarian and, all in all, sounded like a fine group for an idealistic young Protestant man to join.

However, the reality fell short of the ideal. In the fierce competition for land in Ulster, the Catholics all too often outbid the Protestants. As a result, the goal of converting the papists soon devolved to one of driving them out of County Armagh. The Catholics, of course, fought to hold their ancestral land, and the border country was soon in a constant state of tension, with assaults, reprisals and deaths.

The Order spread quickly to North America. The first Canadian meeting was held in Halifax during 1799, but it was in Saint John that the Orangemen first established a lodge. The Saint John lodges drew Protestants from both Irish and non-Irish groups, including many Loyalist descendants, whose grandparents had founded the city.

By 1824 the Saint John lodge obtained its first warrant from Ireland's Orange headquarters. The heavy Irish immigration, both Catholic and Protestant, during the 1820s and 1830s contributed to the Order's spread throughout the colony of New Brunswick. However, during the 1840s, with a vast increase in Roman Catholic immigration and a very depressed economy, violence between the Orange and the Green began.

The Saint John Catholics began the altercations by assaulting a

THE RIGHT REVEREND WILLIAM DOLLARD, D.D.

LATE ROMAN CATHOLIC BISHOP, OF NEW BRUNSWICK.

Bishop William Dollard.

New Brunswick Department of Tourism and Culture

number of Protestants on July 12, 1837, in the spring of 1841 and again on July 12, 1842. However, it was not until Saint Patrick's Day, 1845, that the situation got completely out of hand. Without immediate provocation, some Protestants opened fire on revellers and in the resulting riot at least one Catholic was killed. To make things worse, an all-Protestant grand jury dismissed all charges against the Orange rioters and passed a true bill that led to the conviction of two Catholics for their part in the violence.

Four months later, on July 12, 1845, rioting became general in the Saint John River Valley as Irish Catholics opposed Orange marches, and several from both sides lost their lives. Two years later Orangemen gathered on the outskirts of the Irish Catholic ghetto in northern Saint John and attempted to march through the enclave playing provocative songs such as "Croppies Lie Down." They were driven back by a hail of stones and other debris. Scores were injured in the ensuing riots, and several died but were secretly buried.

Although 1848 was quiet, the next year the last and most murderous riot occurred. On July 12, 1849, the Orangemen again marched into the Catholic ghetto. Gunfire erupted almost immediately and six to eight died before the Royal Army garrison blocked the marchers from returning to the Green area. Apparently the soldiers had initially held back to let the Orangemen discipline the Catholics, who were stereotyped as disloyal troublemakers.

In the trial that followed, the grand jurors released all the Orangemen and convicted only two Catholics. Tension then decreased rapidly as William Dollard, the Catholic bishop of Saint John, gained control over his rebellious parishioners. The Orangemen sought to gain respectability through legislative incorporation and so ceased their provocative marches. However, not until 1875, following six years of bitter sectarian feuding over the effort by Catholics to receive governmental funding for their separate schools, was the Orange Order finally incorporated.

II. Mid-Century

The 1850s marked the height—or, one could say, the depth—of the anti-Catholic movement in the Maritimes. The Orange Order's riots had been one expression of resurgent Protestantism colliding with revived Catholicism. In the 1820s evangelism had reawakened in Ireland as a great Protestant crusade to convert the papists, but shortly thereafter the

British government gave into O'Connell, and the Catholic Emancipation bill was passed. This event, combined with the re-establishment of the Catholic Hierarchy in England at mid-century, and the conversion to Rome of several leading lights of the Anglican Church, shocked the revivalists.

In Nova Scotia the tension expressed itself in a total break between Joseph Howe and the Halifax Irish. The Halifax Roman Catholic Church had become expansive. A second parish had been established in 1847, and two years later both the Sisters of Charity and the Religious of the Sacred Heart had been brought in. The final crisis, however, did not occur until the Crimean War. In 1854 Howe went to Boston and New York to recruit a number of young men, supposedly to work on the Nova Scotia Railway. But William Condon, president of the Charitable Irish Society, believed, apparently correctly, that the men were recruits for the Nova Scotia regiment that was in the Crimean conflict. One April 7, 1855, Condon telegraphed New York with his suspicions. Howe had to make a quick retreat to Halifax and nursed an increasing fury against the "disloyal" Irish.

The next year a riot between the Irish and Scots occurred on the railway north of Halifax. Later, on May 26, 1856, the former British ambassador to Washington, Sir John Crampton, spoke in the Nova Scotian capital and a near riot broke out as some Irish challenged his claims of being illegitimately dismissed by the Americans by pointing out that Crampton had been involved in Howe's recruiting scheme. Howe was almost beside himself with rage and attacked the Irish Catholics once more as traitors. The result was the rending of the Reform, or Liberal, party. Condon was dismissed by the Liberal government from his post with the civil service for violating his term of office with the telegram to New York. Ten Liberals, including two Protestants who represented Catholic districts, crossed the floor and the government fell. The Tories then rubbed salt in the Liberals' wounds by reappointing Condon, but in 1859 the Reformers stormed back into office and Condon was permanently dismissed from the colonial government. However, the Grits had won on an essentially Protestant vote and for the next quarter century would not regain the confidence of the Catholic minority.

III. The Exciting Sixties

The 1860s were exciting times in the Maritimes, and the Irish were strongly involved in the major events. For five years the American Civil

War had raged. Maritimers had a personal interest in the conflict, as many of their sons had gone to serve either the North or the South. After the war was over, the excitement was at home with the Tenant League, the Fenians and the Confederation debate.

Prince Edward Island had suffered land problems almost since it was first surveyed in 1765. A British colony, the island had had foisted upon it a semi-feudal land system that contradicted the generally held ideals of the North American farmer. In almost all cases farmland, which was largely forest covered, had to be rented. The proprietors refused to sell and, as in Ireland, the renters had no protection against arbitrary eviction even after years of labour—cutting, piling and burning trees, pulling stumps and removing stones from the red sandy soil. Upon eviction of his tenants, the landlord had a ready-made farm to rent at a much higher rate than previously, while the broken farmer and his ruined family were forced to start anew.

The response to these occasional and disastrous evictions and the pervasive feeling of insecurity was the Tenant League. This organization was founded in the mid-1860s and apparently took its inspiration from a somewhat similar movement in Ireland more than a decade earlier. The Tenant Union (as it was officially named) united Catholics and Protestants, Irish and Scots, French and English, into a militant but supposedly peaceful organization that attempted to force proprietors to sell on the settlers' terms. Members withheld rents, attacked posses and discouraged opportunists from occupying seized farms.

By the summer of 1865, Queens County was slipping out of the control of the government, and the 16th Berkshire Regiment of Foot was called in from Halifax to restore order and protect the "sacred rights of property." Unfortunately for the government, the 16th had a large number of Irish Catholics and the Tenant League successfully encouraged many of the troops to desert. They were replaced by the much more British 15th Regiment from New Brunswick and the tenant rebellion was suppressed.

However, the land problem was not finally solved for another decade when Prince Edward Island, which had entered Confederation two years earlier in 1873, expropriated the landlords' estates and sold the properties to those whose labour had largely made the land valuable.

One year after the Tenant League had electrified Prince Edward Island, the Fenians galvanized the entire Maritimes, especially Nova Scotia and New Brunswick. The American Fenians had split between those who wanted to attack the British in Ireland and those who wished to hold Canada hostage until the British quit the Emerald Isle. However, as we have seen, the plots in Ireland failed because of British alertness, and so the American Irish found it healthier to fight on on their own side of the Atlantic. As well, they were almost encouraged by the U.S. government, which was rather miffed by the British support of the Confederacy during the recently terminated Civil War. In the end, however, American officials decided it was better not to engage in another conflict and, as a result, they helped the British defuse the situation.

The scare began on March 16, 1866, when a telegram reached Halifax stating that three Fenian ironclad battleships had left New York the previous day to challenge the Grand Battery on Citadel Hill. The Nova Scotian capital was thrown into a panic, especially after a case of revolvers was discovered on a ship in the harbour. On March 21st Mayor Matthew Henry Richie swore about 200 special constables into service, including some local Irish. However, in general the Irish showed mixed feelings about the whole affair. Former alderman John Murphy offered his one hundred or so truck horses to haul government weapons, and Archbishop Thomas Connolly accompanied the British commander, Sir Charles Hastings Doyle when the latter inspected militia draftees. Other Irish were not so enthusiastic. Two balked at being assigned to the militia, one objecting that he, a former American soldier, would not fight his ex-countrymen on the New Brunswick border where the Fenians were massing, but that he would defend Nova Scotia. The other man refused to swear loyalty to Queen Victoria but offered to make his pledge of allegiance to Nova Scotia. So desperate were the officials that both men were accepted.

Almost one week passed and nothing happened. Then from Yarmouth came an alarming telegram that the town was under bombardment. The militias on the South Shore were immediately called into action. Watches were set up on the shores and barrels of pitch were set on the hilltops to signal the arrival of the dreaded Fenian navy. As it turned out, the bombardment was something less than was originally thought. It seems that a few rather bored young men had been out in Yarmouth Harbour in a rowboat firing an old cannon. Such was the sum of the Fenian threat to Nova Scotia.

The real action finally began in April 1866 with the Fenian army fully massed on the New Brunswick-Maine Border. Major General Sir

Major General Sir Charles Hastings Doyle.

Charles Hastings Doyle left for Saint Stephen on the 6th, and three days later HMS *Duncan* sailed into Halifax to take aboard the majority of the 17th Regiment, elements of the Royal Engineers and a battery of the Royal Artillery before sailing for the border.

On April 14th the Fenians finally struck, although not too boldly. They only managed to steal a Union Jack from Indian Island in Passamaquoddy Bay. A week later they returned to the island and burned a few buildings but fled at the approach of some Royal Navy tars. As well, General George Meade of the Grand Army of the Republic confiscated their cache of arms in Maine. So ended the Fenian invasion of the Maritimes, undermined by combined British and American resistance and their own incompetence.

The Fenians' chief impact was on the Confederation debate, especially in New Brunswick. An anti-Confederate government had been elected in that colony the year before the Fenian scare. Both the pro-Confederates and the British government were bitterly opposed to this government and its most important spokesman, Irish-born Timothy Warren Anglin. Using a smear campaign, the pro-Confederates linked Anglin with the Fenians and attacked the supposedly disloyal Irish Catholics of Saint John, while hypocritically courting the pro-Confederate archbishop of Halifax, Thomas Connolly. Connolly was able to influence one of his more anti-Confederate bishops in New Brunswick to end his public opposition to the proposed union. This, combined with the near coup d'état by New Brunswick Lieutenant-Governor Arthur Gordon, destroyed the anti-Confederate government, and thus the colony entered the Dominion at its founding in 1867.

IV. To the Roaring Twenties

During the next half-century the situation of the Irish in the Maritimes changed slowly. The growth of the Orange Order diminished and many Irish, both Orange and Green, left for the "Boston States." The outmigration was especially marked on Cape Breton and Prince Edward islands where the economies were almost perennially depressed. The population fell sharply on Cape Breton, and on Prince Edward Island the Irish proportion decreased from about 25% in the middle of the nineteenth century to just below 20% in 1951. Of course, many Irish did not leave. Instead they concentrated in new industrial areas such as Westville, Moncton and Sydney. The movement of Irish was perhaps most extreme

Orangemen.

Provincial Archives of New Brunswick

in Cape Breton. In 1871 just over half lived in Cape Breton County, while forty years later 90% were there.

Such concentrations of Irish often led to significant changes. For example, the Orange Order became a major force in some of the New Glasgow area towns of Nova Scotia, even though most people seemed to be Scottish Presbyterians. However, the loss of country lodges had tended to offset the town gains, and as a result the growth of the Order was almost static up to the First World War, when membership swelled again.

Other things seemed hardly to change at all. Discrimination continued against Irish Catholics even though they were not so easily branded disloyal. During the slaughter of the First World War, Irish of both persuasions marched resolutely into hell. But the suspicion lingered in Canada that Catholics had not pulled their full weight, especially after Quebec resisted conscription in 1917.

V. Self-Determination

In the period immediately after the First World War, many Irish Canadians, both Orange and Green, experienced their last close involvement with Ireland. This link occurred during the debate over Home Rule, or Irish self-determination. Such freedom had been promised by Britain in 1914, however, mounting resistance in Ulster threw the whole idea into doubt and the First World War suspended its implementation until the peace of 1918. After the war, pressure from both sides mounted. A self-determination league of Canada and Newfoundland was formed in Toronto in July 1920. At its first national convention, Lindsay Crawford, an Ulster-born Protestant, was elected president and he had the strong support of the Roman Catholic bishop of Charlottetown, Henry O'Leary. The next year Crawford toured the Maritimes, where he received a rather rough reception. In Sydney the imperialists packed a hall with British sailors and he was unable to deliver his speech. In Fredericton he was simply barred from speaking by town officials, and in Moncton, with insufficient police protection provided, he was assaulted, his pockets were rifled and he was made to kiss the Union Jack.

However, with the partition of Ireland and the resultant civil war there, the self-determination league lost its relevance and folded, and so the politics of Ireland slowly faded in importance among most of its descendents in the Maritimes.

VI. The Antigonish Movement

As the 1920s moved on, much of the world was caught up in speculative fever and many huge fortunes were made, at least on paper. The reckoning came on October 26, 1929, when the New York Stock Exchange crashed and millions saw their wealth disappear.

However, eastern Nova Scotia already knew about economic depressions, having been in one since the early 1920s. As a result there was great poverty and some malnutrition. One attempt to solve these problems was the Antigonish Movement.

As early as 1921, Father James Tompkins of St. Francis Xavier University had established a people's school on campus, and seven years later his fellow Margaree Valley Irishman, Father Moses Coady helped to set up an extension department at the university to spread Tompkins' ideas. Thus began the Antigonish Movement. The department stimulated farmers and fishermen to educate themselves and showed them how to set up cooperatives and credit unions. Although looked upon with

Rev. James J. Tompkins.

Dr. Moses M. Coady.

suspicion by many as too socialistic, the movement gained the support of some high churchmen, including Prince Edward Island-born James Cardinal McGuigan, then archbishop of Regina.

In the 1930s the Antigonish Movement extended its activities to industrial Cape Breton where the communists were making good progress because of their willingness to stand with workers even unto death. A labour school was established there, and with the rise of the Cooperative Commonwealth Federation (CCF), which came to have much in common with the Antigonish Movement, the Marxist influence eventually diminished.

In 1959, when Coady died, an international institute was established at the university in his memory, and the movement moved into the Third World, but it faded in its home area, becoming more a social service agency than a people's reform movement.

By the middle of the twentieth century, Irish Catholics had largely been accepted as true Canadians, as the Orangemen had been seventy-five years earlier. However, there were still a few exceptions. The prominent Nova Scotian genealogist Terrence Punch reports that when he started researching the Irish side of his family more than a generation ago, the late provincial archivist rebuffed him, saying the Irish had been trouble wherever they went! Fortunately the assistant archivist was more open-minded and Punch was able to begin his work.

CHAPTER 4
Contributions to the Maritimes and Canada

As individuals, and through their institutions, the Irish have played a very important role in shaping the character of the Maritimes. Many Maritime universities and many of the Christian churches in the region were founded by Irishmen. Most of the original colonial governors were of Irish birth or descent, many businessmen have claimed Irish origins, and how could a people known for the gift of the gab not produce literary figures? The Irish also had at least their share of athletes and produced or participated in a number of important social organizations.

I. Religion and Education

Until recently, a very close relationship existed between organized religion and education. Although a significant majority of the Maritime Irish were Catholic, there were also Anglicans, Baptists, Methodists and Presbyterians among them in significant numbers, and this was especially true in New Brunswick where non-Catholic Irish actually formed a small majority. Most of these Protestant Irish groups, like the Catholics, formed denominational colleges.

Anglicans represented the official religion in these early colonies and were the first off the mark. Bishop Charles Inglis (whose Irish nickname was Paddy) set up the oldest Canadian college, King's, at Windsor, Nova Scotia, in 1789, to train clergy for the Church of England in the Maritime colonies. King's degrees were first recognized in 1802, and after 124 years the school moved to Halifax to be associated with Dalhousie University. The transfer was the result of a disastrous fire in 1920 and of enticement by the Carnegie Corporation, which was trying to form a federated Maritime university in Halifax. The University of

Saint Mary's University in the 1950s.

King's College was a founding member of the Atlantic School of Theology and today hosts an important school of journalism.

During the same year King's received its charter (1802), the foundations of Saint Mary's University were laid in Halifax. That year the Catholic bishop, Edmund Burke, started a junior seminary at his residence. However, it was not until 1841 that the college was chartered. In a precarious condition for decades, Saint Mary's did not attain stability until the Irish Christian Brothers took over in 1913. Twenty-seven years later the Jesuits were brought in, and they ran the school until 1970 when the formal link with the archdiocese of Halifax was ended. Today, Saint Mary's is a nominally Christian university noted for its athletic prowess and its school of business. The school also has the only Irish Studies program in the Atlantic provinces, with courses in language, literature and history.

In the late 1830s both the Irish Baptists and Irish Methodists founded their own colleges. The first is Acadia in Wolfville, Nova Scotia. Edward Manning, whose family had formerly been Catholic, joined the Baptists in 1789, at the time of Henry Alline's "New Light Movement," a religious revival that swept the Maritimes after having affected New England. In 1828 Manning helped to found a Baptist

Mount Allison University at the turn of the century.

school in Wolfville, and a decade later an offshoot became Acadia. Despite its religious orientation, the university has never imposed any sectarian tests. Acadia was officially recognized in 1841 and today still has a school of divinity despite the fact that it is not controlled by a Baptist board of governors.

The third originally Irish Protestant college is Mount Allison, founded by Charles Allison, a prominent merchant of Ulster Scots descent who had left the Church of England to become a Methodist. Allison bought land and established a school in Sackville, New Brunswick, at his own expense. In 1843 he opened Mount Allison Academy, and a ladies' college was established about a decade later. In 1858 Mount Allison's degrees received official recognition and in 1875 it granted the first degree ever to be received by a woman anywhere in the British Empire. Today the university has a noted fine arts and music program and maintains links with the United Church although it is not controlled by that denomination.

One Maritime women's college also has Irish roots—Mount Saint Vincent University, staffed by the Sisters of Charity. Bishop William

Walsh brought the nuns from New York in 1849, and twenty-four years later the "Charities" established an academy that became Mount Saint Vincent. There they educated the young ladies of Halifax. Despite serious problems with one stubborn Irish-Canadian archbishop, William Hanlan, the school survived and in 1914 started offering degrees in cooperation with Dalhousie. Eleven years later "the Mount" offered its own degrees and became the first independent women's college in the British Empire. Today, although the school is still nominally directed by the Sisters of Charity, it has a significant number of male students but maintains the tradition of providing Roman Catholic education to those students who want it.

The last institution of higher learning in the Maritimes founded by Irish is St. Thomas University in Chatham, New Brunswick, which was established in 1910 by Bishop Thomas Barry. The school was originally staffed by the Basilian Fathers. It was not until 1934 that degree granting powers were obtained, and in 1964 the college moved to Fredericton where it situated itself on the University of New Brunswick campus in a relationship similar to that between King's and Dalhousie in Halifax. It has continued its association with the Irish, and in March 1989 St. Thomas was the site of the annual meeting of the Canadian Association of Irish Studies.

II. Politics

Some of the early governors of the Maritime colonies were members of the Irish Ascendency. In Nova Scotia there was John Parr, in New Brunswick Thomas Carleton and on Prince Edward Island Walter Patterson. Although their names may not sound Irish, Irish-born they were, and it was their class that tried to set up the Irish parliament in Dublin in the late 1700s.

With the move toward responsible government, new leaders took power. These were the first elected colonial premiers, and many were Irish. John Boyle Uniacke was the head of the first responsible government in the British Empire overseas, formed on February 2, 1848, in Nova Scotia. On Prince Edward Island, Edward Palmer, an opponent of responsible government (and it seems just about any other progressive measure) was elected premier six years after the implementation of that form of government.

However, up to the last quarter of the nineteenth century, even though some had been Irish, premiers and most governors had been

W.W. Sullivan.

Public Archives of Prince Edward Island

Protestant. Finally in 1879, W.W. Sullivan, an Irish Catholic, was elected premier of Prince Edward Island. After this the election of Catholics became somewhat easier. However, as late as 1954 religion seemed to play a political role as Harold Connolly, the interim Liberal leader in Nova Scotia, was defeated at a leadership convention. The Protestant candidates were accused of "ganging up" on Connolly, the only Catholic contender and the leading candidate. As a result, it took

Contributions to the Maritimes and Canada   47

John Sparrow Thompson.

Owen Connolly.

the Grits a decade and a half to regain the Catholic vote.

The Maritime Irish reached the pinnacle of Canadian politics but once. John Sparrow Thompson of Halifax, who was called by Sir John A. Macdonald his greatest discovery, had been appointed to the federal cabinet as minister of justice in 1885. Thompson, a Protestant friend of Archbishop Thomas Connolly, named a son after the prelate and joined the Catholic Church. He became prime minister of Canada in 1892 but died less than three years later at age 49.

III. Business

The Irish, like other immigrant groups, often moved into business after enough capital had been saved. In Halifax the names of William Stairs and Isaac Morrow, John and Michael Tobin and Patrick Power were well known. Peter Smyth was important in Cape Breton, as were some of the Archibalds originally from Truro. In New Brunswick, William Kelly of Moncton, Henry O'Leary of Richibucto, "Boss" Gibson of Marysville and the Burchills of the Miramichi were prominent, and Owen Connolly was the chief Irish merchant on Prince Edward Island.

These men often gave their money to good causes, such as higher education. Charles Allison, as mentioned, was the founder of Mount Allison University, Peter Smyth helped St. Francis Xavier and Owen Connolly set up scholarships at Saint Dunstan's University (later one of the constituents of the University of Prince Edward Island) for poor but talented Irish boys. Sometimes, however, the gifts were not accessible. Patrick Power gave money to the archdiocese of Halifax to educate Catholic boys, and Saint Mary's College expected to get it but ended up with very little. After years of court battles over certain stipulations, namely the role of the Jesuits, it was decreed that only a small part would go to Saint Mary's, and that is used today to support the chaplaincy at the university.

IV. Literature

The Irish have begun to make their mark in literature. In the nineteenth century perhaps their most prominent writer was Cornelius O'Brien, the Prince Edward Island-born archbishop of Halifax. Shy and retiring, he only seemed comfortable with children but was a poet of note and also wrote religious works such as *The Philosophy of the Bible Vindicated.*

In the twentieth century the outstanding name seems to be that of Alden Nowlan, the Nova Scotian-born poet of New Brunswick. An apparent relation to the political Nowlans of the Annapolis Valley, he moved to New Brunswick at 19 years of age and rapidly gained a reputation for his prose. Nowlan won the Governor General's prize in 1967 for his *Bread, Wine and Salt*. He also wrote *Playing the Jesus Game* and *Various Persons Named Kevin O'Brien*. Nowlan died in his early fifties in 1983.

Prince Edward Island has produced several women writers of note. Lucy Clarkin was a poet, and a writer for *Saturday Night* and the Montreal *Star*, and Katherine Hughes was a noted biographer. Hughes wrote the biographies of her uncle Cornelius O'Brien and of Father LaCombe, missionary to the Cree and Blackfoot. However, her biography of Canadian Pacific Railway magnate Cornelius Van Horne was not released under her own name apparently because Van Horne's family objected to her pro-Irish politics, especially her support of the self-determination league.

More recently, scholars such as Cyril Byrne have started to make their mark in historical literature.

V. Sports

The "fighting Irish" naturally produced a number of good athletes, both male and female. At the turn of the century, Halifax rower John O'Neill, a veteran of the Boer War and later of the North West Mounted Police, was prominent. In 1908 he was second in the North American rowing championship, and the next year he won it.

A quarter of a century later the name on everyone's lips was Aileen Meagher. Born in Edmonton, Alberta, of Haligonian parents, she returned to the Nova Scotian capital as a child and attended Dalhousie University. Meagher was invited to try out for the 1932 Olympics and four years later in Berlin, as part of the 400-yard women's relay team, she won the bronze medal. In later years this school teacher became a well-known semi-abstract artist travelling much of the world, including Ireland, where she did a number of drawings. Saint Mary's Irish Studies program has many of these today. Meagher died in Halifax in 1985.

More recently the star was Prince Edward Island's Anna Pendergast, daughter of well-known athlete "Big Jim" Pendergast. She attended Dalhousie University as an all-star basketball player and became the first woman to score more than 1,000 points in her college career. As

Alden Nowlan.

New Brunswick Department of Tourism and Culture

a player on the national team she won a bronze medal in the 1986 Olympics.

VI. The Charitable Irish Societies

The earliest of the Maritime Irish philanthropic groups is the Charitable Irish Society of Halifax, founded in 1786 as a gentlemen's club which assigned itself the duty of aiding the destitute and the business of entertaining its own members. These men were both Protestant and Catholic, and included such early notables as the governor of the colony, John Parr; the first Catholic priest in Halifax, Reverend James Jones; Lawrence Kavanaugh, father to the first Catholic to sit in a British parliament since the Reformation; and Richard John Uniacke, a sire to the first premier of Nova Scotia, James Boyle Uniacke.

During the 1840s the Charitable Irish Society helped with famine relief in Ireland and supported repeal. Progressively the membership became more Catholic, and during the Crimean War its president engaged in a famous debate with Joseph Howe over conscription. One last gasp of radicalism took hold of the society during the 1920s when at least some members supported Irish self-determination. Today the Charitable Irish Society is conservative, being middle class, middle-aged and middle of the road, but a few members still refuse to stand for the toast to the Queen.

A second major charitable Irish organization was the Saint Patrick's Society of Saint John, founded in 1819. It was similar to the Halifax group, but clearly Protestant from its beginning and for decades following. It championed the Irish as loyal Britons. More radical and Catholic was the Saint John Sons of Erin, a group that resembled the Charitable Irish Society of Halifax at mid-century during the latter's anti-British phase. They supported repeal but met most often, curiously, at the hotel of James Nethery, an Orangeman, where they discussed Irish problems over many a bottle. The Sons ran afoul of the local Catholic bishop, William Dollard, in a dispute over lay control of the parish similar to that which had taken place in Halifax more than half a century earlier. They were quickly brought to heel. Today the Sons of Erin is extinct, but the Saint Patrick's Society still meets.

On Prince Edward Island, the Beneficial Irish Society was founded in 1825 and, like the Charitable Irish Society, it was both Catholic and Protestant. The group had goals similar to those of the Halifax society and met in a Roman Catholic chapel despite Ascendency names among them, such as Palmer, Longworth and DesBrisay. As time passed, they too became more radical and more Catholic. By the middle of the nineteenth century they generally supported repeal and at least some were members of the Tenant League. Like the Halifax society, the Beneficial Irish Society had sympathy for self-determination under the leadership of the local Catholic bishop, Henry O'Leary, who was on the national committee. Today it still organizes a Saint Patrick's Day parade followed by Mass at Saint Dunstan's Cathedral, engages in charity and brings in speakers on things Irish.

In 1990 the Irish Association of Nova Scotia (An Cumann) was founded. It meets at St. Paul's Roman Catholic Church in Herring Cove and aims to gain a wider Nova Scotia membership than the Charitable Irish Society of Halifax. Its members are younger and many speak Irish, either learned as natives or through courses at Saint Mary's University. The association plans to have a strong educational program.

CHAPTER 5
Prominent Individuals

Who were the well-known Maritime Irish? Many have already been mentioned, at least in passing, on the previous pages. People such as Sir John Thompson, Richard John Uniacke and John Boyle Uniacke, Sir W.W. Sullivan and Bishop Charles Inglis dominated the eighteenth and nineteenth centuries. In more recent times we have had Bishop Henry O'Leary, Aileen Meagher and Alden Nowlan. Here we shall look at few more of the many men and women of Irish descent who have helped to shape the Maritimes and/or Canada.

Thomas Carleton

The first Lieutenant-Governor of New Brunswick, Thomas Carleton was born in Ireland about 1735. A brother to Sir Guy Carleton, the governor of Quebec, he served in the Seven Years' War and along with Russians fought the Turks. In 1776 he came to Canada and was appointed as governor of New Brunswick on July 28, 1784. Being of Irish Ascendency stock, he supported the Loyalists but was eventually worn out by the opposition of the Assembly Rights Party and retired to England in 1803. Nonetheless, he held onto the governorship as a sinecure until his death on February 2, 1817.

The Archibalds

This famous Nova Scotian family is descended from Ulster Scots who moved from Londonderry, Ireland, to Londonderry, New Hampshire, perhaps as early as 1720. In 1762 they came to the Maritimes among the New England Planters who took over the evacuated Acadian farms in the Londonderry, Nova Scotia, area. Some of the Archibalds

Thomas Carleton.

Sir Adams George Archibald.

were sympathetic to the American Revolution and it is even said that Samuel George William Archibald, who later became chief justice of Prince Edward Island, was christened Samuel George Washington Archibald.

Perhaps the best known of the family was Sir Adams George Archibald, who was born in Truro, Nova Scotia, on May 18, 1814, and was a delegate to the Charlottetown, Quebec and London conferences that created Canada. Later he was Lieutenant-Governor of Manitoba and then succeeded Joseph Howe as Lieutenant-Governor of Nova Scotia. He died in Truro on December 14, 1892.

Charles Archibald (1845-1929), a member of the Sydney branch of the family, became president of the Bank of Nova Scotia in 1918, and while his wife, Edith Jessie (1854-1936), also an Archibald, was a well-known suffragette. A relative of Charles, Doctor Edgar Spinney Archibald of Yarmouth (1885-1968) was head of the Dominion Experimental Station in Ottawa from 1919 to 1951.

Sir Edmund Archibald helped to establish responsible government in Newfoundland. Doctor Francis Archibald (1899-) was head of research at Standard Oil's largest refinery. Judge John Archibald (1843-1932) ruled that Blacks had the right to occupy orchestra seats in Nova Scotia theatres, and Raymond Archibald (1875-1955) was the first English speaker to win a doctorate at the University of Strasbourg in France.

Today the family is represented by Gordon Archibald, retired president of the Maritime Telephone and Telegraph Corporation, and his son, George Archibald, Conservative member for Kings North in the Nova Scotia legislature.

Archbishop Thomas Connolly

The best known of Maritime Catholic prelates during the nineteenth century, Thomas Connolly was born in County Cork in 1815. He came to Halifax as a priest at age 27 and within a decade was the bishop of Saint John. He was described by his superior, Archbishop William Walsh of Halifax, as multilingual, kind, outstanding in character, but too easy with dispensations and too friendly with the laity.

In New Brunswick, Connolly established an orphanage and brought in the Sisters of Charity, claimed precedence over the Anglican bishop and, despite his disagreements with Timothy Warren Anglin over Confederation, was quite popular among the Irish, though others thought him to be arrogant.

Right Rev. Thomas Louis Connolly.

National Archives of Canada

Supported by churchmen on both sides of the Atlantic, including Archbishop (and later Cardinal) Paul Cullen of Dublin, and New York's first Catholic archbishop, John Hughes, Connolly was elevated to the archdiocese of Halifax in 1859 and managed to smooth the rough waters caused by the anti-Catholic politics of Howe and others. He bitterly

Prominent Individuals   59

Timothy Warren Anglin.

New Brunswick Department of Tourism and Culture

opposed the Fenians and, as previously mentioned, used his influence to tone down the anti-Confederate musings of one of his New Brunswick bishops.

Connolly threw himself into the Confederation debate and worked so efficiently that he has been deemed the "Godfather of Confederation." During this time he tried but failed to secure support for a separate provincial school system for Catholics. However, he accepted a de facto separate school system when it was offered.

During the late 1860s Connolly was troubled by the Pope's claims to infallibility in matters of faith and morals and felt the Pope had made an inopportune declaration. Connolly even offered a monetary prize to anyone who could find a scriptural basis for such a claim. There were no takers. Despite this the vote on the declaration easily passed in Rome, but Connolly had already left for Halifax rather than vote against the Pope.

Connolly died on July 27, 1876, known for his fights with the anti-Catholic Howe ad the anti-Protestant Pius IX, and for his friendship with Presbyterian minister George Munroe Grant and Prime Minister John Sparrow Thompson.

Timothy Warren Anglin

Born in Clonakilty, County Cork, on August 31, 1822, Timothy Warren Anglin moved to Saint John in 1849 after the Great Famine ruined his family's fortunes. A gifted journalist, he published the *Freeman* for many years in that city and used it to oppose Confederation and its chief supporter Thomas D'Arcy McGee.

As the Confederation debate was raging, the Fenians raided New Brunswick. Because Anglin was not as opposed to them as McGee, the pro-Confederates were able not only to defeat him but also the government in which he served as minister without portfolio.

However, in 1867 Anglin was elected to the Canadian House of Commons and served as its speaker for five years. He also involved himself in the separate school debate in New Brunswick during the 1870s, but to no avail as the Catholics lost. Eventually a compromise was reached and a de facto Catholic school system was established. The year 1883 saw Anglin in Toronto, having closed the *Freeman*. He then wrote for the Toronto *Globe*. However, after four years his work became spotty, and he died in reduced circumstances in Toronto on May 3, 1896.

His progeny carried on. His son Frank was chief justice of Canada

Katherine Hughes.

and his daughter Margaret was a noted Shakespearean actress. A grandson, a retired Basilian priest in Toronto, is the founder of the Anglin Collection, one of two major depositories of Catholic history in Canada, at the University of Saskatchewan.

Katherine Hughes

Born at Emerald, Prince Edward Island, in 1876, Katherine Hughes became a pro-Irish writer and lecturer. She reported for the Montreal *Star* and the *Edmonton Bulletin*. In 1913 she was appointed assistant to the Alberta agent general in London and was able to travel to Ireland, something that changed her life. There Hughes was caught up in the self-determination movement and supported De Valera's Sinn Fein party. After returning to Canada, she lectured for the Self-Determination for Ireland League of Canada and Newfoundland, touring the Canadian West as well as her native Maritimes. On Prince Edward Island she was associated with the pro-Irish bishop Henry O'Leary, but the league soon became irrelevant and she moved to the United States to continue her writings. She died at the height of her powers in New York City on April 27, 1925. She was only 48.

James Charles McGuigan

Born at Hunter River, Prince Edward Island, on November 26, 1884, James Charles McGuigan's ancestors came from County Monaghan just before the Great Famine. A brilliant student, he took his doctorate in divinity with great distinction at Laval University in Quebec City and became possibly the youngest archbishop in the Roman Catholic Church in 1930 when appointed to Regina, Saskatchewan, at only 35 years of age.

He was just in time for both the Great Drought and the Great Depression. Temporarily overwhelmed by the seemingly insurmountable problems, he broke down but recovered and worked with great vigour to overcome the archdiocesan debt and to keep the schools and churches open. Among other things, he travelled to central Canada begging for food and money.

Rome was so impressed that it handed him an even bigger problem, Toronto, a challenge that he tried unsuccessfully to turn down. Here he again gave of himself totally, expanding the separate school system in the face of opposition led by the Orange Order, He built dozens of

Harold Connolly.

Alan Blakeney.

churches and expanded the Catholic hospital system. In 1945 he became the first Canadian Cardinal.

It was said that this shy man could dominate any gathering with his wit and brilliance, but he had no desire to be Pope. In his old age he attended the Second Vatican Council but suffered a massive stroke in 1965, the year the gathering ended. McGuigan was confined, speechless and crippled, to his home where he died nine years later on April 8, 1974, having given his life to the Church.

Harold Connolly

Born in Sydney, Nova Scotia, on September 8, 1901, Connolly was first a newspaperman and later rose to become premier of Nova Scotia. His Irish ancestors had come to the province through New Brunswick.

Connolly's defeat as interim premier at the Liberal convention in 1954 split the party. The leading candidate and successor to the Scottish-Catholic Angus L. Macdonald, Connolly was rejected when the other candidates, all of whom were Protestant, united against him. This was the last apparent gasp of anti-Catholicism in Nova Scotian politics and helped keep the Liberals from office for most of a generation.

Connolly became a Senator on 1955 and died in Halifax on May 17, 1980. His daughter, Sharon Carstairs became leader of the Manitoba Liberal party.

Alan Blakeney

Born in Bridgewater, Nova Scotia, on September 7, 1925, Alan Blakeney's ancestors had come from Northern Ireland to South Carolina in 1762 and moved to Nova Scotia sixteen years later. A graduate of Dalhousie and Oxford universities, Blakeney was called to the Saskatchewan Bar in 1950. He became a socialist depite his conservative upbringing in Bridgewater and in 1971 was elected New Democratic Party premier of Saskatchewan, serving until 1982. His administration was nationally known and admired and he supported the idea of a decentralized federal government. In 1987 Blakeney retired from politics and now teaches law at Osgoode Hall in Toronto.

CHAPTER 6
Irish in the Maritimes in the 1990s

Today the Irish are generally indistinguishable from the general population. They share the same materialistic outlook and religious indifference of the majority, and they celebrate Saint Paddy's Day by drinking green beer and purchasing toy leprechauns. They have "arrived," but what price have they paid?

But not all is lost. Despite the commercialized Irish music at places such as O'Carroll's in Halifax and the Old Dublin Pub in Charlottetown, traditional and educational activities for those who wish to move past the merely superficial can still be found in the Maritimes. Irish festivals have been established in recent years, the best known being that held on the Miramichi in mid-July at Chatham, New Brunswick. This event is somewhat commercialized and a bit sectarian, with a Mass and no evident Protestant ceremonies, but the organizers also make an effort to promote genealogical, community history, Irish-language and literary sessions. And there are plans for a multi-million-dollar Irish theme park on the Miramichi.

Much less well known is the festival at Mill River, Prince Edward Island, held in early July. Here an attempt to produce a more genuine Irish display is made, and one scholar has said the atmosphere there was one of the rare occasions that made him feel as if he were really in Ireland.

On the academic side, a serious effort has been made to organize a chair of Irish Studies at Saint Mary's University in Halifax. Professor Cyril Byrne, coordinated the effort and an Irish speaker, Professor Padraig O'Siadhail, was appointed to the chair. Courses are offered at the undergraduate level in Irish literature and language. Scottish is also

Cyril Byrne

Saint Mary's University

Brendan O'Grady

Mary Clancy

PHOTO 67

Frank McKenna

Province of New Brunswick

68   The Irish

occasionally offered, as is Welsh. The chair would like to conduct a computerized survey of the Irish in Nova Scotia, which would complement the work being done by Professor Peter Toner in New Brunswick and Professor Brendan O'Grady on Prince Edward Island.

Publications on the Irish also continue to flourish. In New Brunswick, Peter Toner has edited the first serious work on the province's Irish, *New Ireland Remembered*. On Prince Edward Island, Brendan O'Grady has edited Irish editions of the *Abegweit Review* and included his ground-breaking paper on the Monaghan settlers in the first volume. He is also writing a history of the Prince Edward Island Irish to 1880. In Nova Scotia, Terrence Punch has produced many articles, especially about the Halifax Irish.

Biographies are also being produced. Padriag O'Siadhail is writing a literary biography of Catherine Hughes; Robert Bedard is researching the life of Archbishop John T. McNally of Halifax; and this writer is working on the biography of Cardinal McGuigan. Such publications are often associated with conferences held at local universities. For example, Saint Mary's University hosted the Second North American Congress of Celtic Studies during the summer of 1989, and a volume of relevant papers is expected to be published from this.

Politically, the Irish are still prominent. Frank McKenna has been the premier of New Brunswick, and Mary Clancy has represented Halifax at Ottawa. The Donahoes have been a force in Halifax, and Irish in the judiciary have included Supreme Court Associate Justice Mark MacGuigan in Ottawa, Prince Edward Island Supreme Court Justice George Mullally and Nova Scotia Supreme Court Justice Patrick Curran. The Irish have recently held many Maritime ecclesiastical positions. For example, Monsignor James Hayes has been the Roman Catholic Archbishop of Halifax and Reverend W.E. O'Grady has been the administrator-treasurer of the United Baptist Convention of the Atlantic provinces.

While the O'Learys no longer operate in Richibucto, New Brunswick, and the Owen Connollys no longer do business in Charlottetown, Stairs and Morrow still exist in Halifax and new companies bearing Irish names have sprung up. In Saint John the McNultys operate a traditional Irish business, cartage; the O'Briens are electricians in the same port city; and Summerside, P.E.I., has McCloskey's Appliances.

The Orange Order still exists, but in a much reduced form. In Charlottetown it has so changed that not only lodge meetings but French immersion lessons take place in the lodge hall. New Brunswick has somewhat more Orange Order activity, while in Nova Scotia the lodges are almost unknown.

What does the future hold for the Maritime Irish? People who trace their roots back to the Emerald Isle will continue to make significant contributions to life in the Maritimes. With the usual shortage of of jobs down east, however, more emigration might be expected. Funding for Irish studies may be less forthcoming as Irish-descended Prime Minister Brian Mulroney cuts spending to balance the federal budget, but the foundations for serious studies of the Maritime Irish have been laid, and individual and university-funded efforts will continue. As a result, more publications on the Maritime Irish should become available in the years ahead.

Bibliography

Acheson, T.W. "The Irish Community in Saint John, 1815-1850." In *New Ireland Remembered: Historical Essays on the Irish in New Brunswick*, Peter Toner, Ed. Fredericton: New Ireland Press, 1989.

Acheson, T.W. *Saint John: The Making of a Colonial Urban Community*. UToronto: University of Toronto Press, 1985.

Acheson, T.W. "The National Policy and the Industrialization of the Maritimes, 1880 - 1928" *Acadiensis* 1.2 (1972): #3-28.

Baker, William M. "Squelching the Disloyal Fenian-Sympathizing Brood: T.W. Anglin and Confederation in New Brunswick, 1865-66." In *New Ireland Remembered*.

Baker, William M. "Turning the Spit: Timothy Anglin and the Roasting of D'Arcy McGee." In *The Untold Story: The Irish in Canada*, Robert O'Driscoll and Lorna Reynolds, eds. Toronto: Celtic Arts of Canada, 1988.

Baum, Gregory. *Catholics and Canadian Socialism: Political Thought in the Thirties and Forties*. Toronto: James Lorimer, 1980.

Byrne, Cyril J. "The D'Arcy McGee Chair of Irish Studies." *Nova Scotia Historical Review* 6.1 (1986): 36-40.

Byrne, Cyril J. "A Letter to Father William Phalen, 1786." *Nova Scotia Historical Review* 6.1 (1986): 63-74.

Cameron, James M. "Fenian Times in Nova Scotia." *Collections of the Nova Scotia Historical Society* 37. Halifax: Kentville Publishing, 1970.

Davis, Richard. "Irish Nationalism in Manitoba, 1870-1922." In *The Untold Story.*

Dobbs, Kildare. "Newfoundland and the Maritimes: An Overview." In *The Untold Story.*

Flewelling, Mrs. R.G. "Immigration to and Emigration from Nova Scotia, 1839-51." *Collections of the Nova Scotia Historical Society* 28 (1961): 75-97.

Hannington, J. Brian. *Every Popish Person: The Story of Roman Catholicism in Nova Scotia and the Church of Halifax, 1604-1984.* Halifax: Archdiocese of Halifax, 1984.

Hind, Henry Youle. *The University of Kings College, Windsor, Nova Scotia, 1790 - 1890.* New York: Church Review, 1890.

Houston, Cecil J., and William J. Smith. *The Sash Canada Wore: A Historical Geography of the Orange Order in Canada.* Toronto: University of Toronto Press, 1980.

Harvey, Robert P. "Black Beans, Banners and Banquets: The Charitable Irish Society of Halifax at Two Hundred." *Nova Scotia Historical Review* 6.1 (1986): 16-35.

Johnson, Ray. *A Glance Backward.* Pickering, Ontario: privately printed, 1988.

Kee, Robert. *Ireland, A History.* Boston: Little Brown, 1982.

MacDonald, G. Edward. *The History of Saint Dunstan's University 1855 - 1956.* Charlottetown: Board of Governors of Saint Dunstan's University and P.E.I. Heritage Foundation.

MacGuigan, Mark R. *Island Ancestors*. Ottawa: privately printed, 1986.

McGuigan, Peter T. "From Wexford and Monaghan: The Lot 22 Irish." *Abegweit Review* 5.1 (1985): 61-96.

McGuigan, Peter T. "James Charles McGuigan: The First Cardinal from English Canada." In *The Untold Story*.

McGuigan, Peter T. "The Lot 61 Irish: Settlement and Stabilization." *Abegweit Review* 6.1 (1988): 38-62.

MacKenzie, A.A. *The Irish in Cape Breton*. Antigonish: Formac, 1979.

MacKinnon, D.A., and A.B. Warbarton. *Past and Present of Prince Edward Island*. Charlottetown: Bowan, 1906.

Marble, Allan E. *Nova Scotians at Home and Abroad*. Hantsport, N.S.: Lancelot, 1989.

Moody, Barry M. *Gives Us an A: An Acadia Album*. Wolfville: Acadia University, 1988.

Morgan, Robert. "Poverty, Wretchedness and Misery: The Great Famine in Cape Breton, 1845-51." *Nova Scotia Historical Review* 6.1 (1986): 88-104.

Murphy, Terrence. "The Emergence of Maritime Catholicism: 1781-1830." *Acadiensis* 13.2 (1984): 29-49.

O'Grady, Brendan. "The Monaghan Settlers" *Abegweit Review* 4.1 (1983): 51-80.

Punch, Terrence. "Finding Our Irish." *Nova Scotia Historical Review* 6.1 (1986): 41-62.

Punch, Terrence. *Irish Halifax: The Immigrant Generation*. Ethnic Heritage Series, No. 5. Halifax: Saint Mary's University, n.d.

Punch, Terrence. "The Repeal List of 1843." *The Island Magazine* 20 (1986): 29-37.

Reid, John G. *Mount Allison University: A History to 1963*. Toronto: University of Toronto Press, 1984.

See, Scott W. "The Fortunes of the Orange Order in 19th Century New Brunswick." In *New Ireland Remembered*.

See, Scott W. "The Orange Order and Social Violence in Mid-Nineteenth Century New Brunswick." In *New Ireland Remembered*.

Spray, William A. "The Irish in the Miramichi." In *New Ireland Remembered*.

Spray, William A. "Reception of the Irish in New Brunswick." In *New Ireland Remembered*.

Toner, Peter M. "Foundations of the Catholic Church in English-Speaking New Brunswick." In *New Ireland Remembered*.

Toner, Peter M. "Introduction." In *New Ireland Remembered*.

Toner, Peter M. "The Irish of New Brunswick at Mid Century: The 1851 Census." In *New Ireland Remembered*.

Young, Alexander. *Beyond Heroes: A Sport History of Nova Scotia*. Hantsport, N.S.: Lancelot, 1980.

Wagg, Phyllis C. "Father William Phalen: An Irish Troublemaker in Arichat." *Nova Scotia Historical Review* 6.1 (1986): 75-87.

Whalen, James. "Allmost as Bad as Ireland: The Experience of an Irish Famine Immigrant in Canada, Saint John, 1847." In *The Untold Story*.

Woodham-Smith, Cecil. *The Great Hunger: Ireland 1845 - 1849*. London: Hamish Hamilton, 1962.